PAIR-IT BOOKS®

Zoo Animals

Written by Mary E. Pearson

STECK-VAUGHN
ELEMENTARY · SECONDARY · ADULT · LIBRARY

A Harcourt Company

www.steck-vaughn.com

A monkey swings.

A kangaroo hops.

A polar bear swims.

A lion climbs.

A turtle crawls.

A giraffe runs.

Children ride!